Dr. Chuck Tingle's Complete Guide To Romance

CHUCK TINGLE

Copyright © 2015 Chuck Tingle

All rights reserved.

ISBN: 1514740737
ISBN-13: 978-1514740736

DEDICATION

To my sweet, sweet Barbara, who still haunts my dreams from beneath that frozen lake.

CONTENTS

1	Introduction	1
2	The Approach	Pg 3
3	First Date	Pg 10
4	Locking It Down	Pg 13
5	Non-Traditional Relationships	Pg 17
6	Marriage	Pg 22
7	Romance Tips And Tricks	Pg 26
8	Sex	Pg 32
9	All Is Fair In Love And War	Pg 37
10	Final Thoughts	Pg 40

INTRODUCTION

Romance has many faces, a quick, flirtatious look from a handsome dinosaur or a long-term bigfoot relationship that has stood the test of time. Sometimes love can be hard to see even though it's right in front of you, while other times I can hit you like a brick, knocking you off your feet with the weight of it's ferocious presence. Love can be sneaky, but it certainly cannot be ignored.

With so many ways of looking at such a universal feeling, it's no wonder that people find the birds and the bees to be so confusing.

Many people find unicorns to be flighty and forgetful, yet somehow they retain relationships longer than any other creature while still reporting incredibly high occurrences of sexually liberal exploration. Meanwhile, dinosaurs may have a hard time shaking the bad boy stereotype that seems to haunt them, but beyond the scaly exterior there is a care and honesty rivaled only by close friends and loved ones. As we all know, living vehicles can have a mind of their own sometimes, yet they are often incredibly loyal to their partners.

Suffice to say, things are hardly as they first seem in the world of romance.

Growing up in the small town of Home of Truth, Utah, I wouldn't have seemed a likely candidate to author a book on unraveling the locks of love.

I was an only child, born to parents who were incredibly faithful people, following the word of the lord to a T and never questioning his message. Their faith was so unshakable, in fact, that when the rest of the town pulled up shop and left in a cloud of dust, my parents decided to stay behind and continue to wait for their prayers of salvation to be answered.

The constant alone time provided me with plenty of space to think, looking inward to my own imagination for entertainment. It's here that I first found the beginning sparks of creativity that would eventually become my carrier as a world renowned and best selling romance author.

I was home schooled my entire life, but my parents taught me plenty about the world, at least enough to get my excitement going at the prospect of meeting a handsome unicorn or a devilishly cool talking plane. However, when it came to romance they were very strict in their message; no can do, buster.

Eventually, when our house burned down in the great fire and I made the solo trek to Billings, Montana, I was forced to learn about love on my own. Equipped with the knowledge I had been raised with on, a quick wit, and a knack for spells and magic, I started a family and carved out a fantastic life for myself here in big sky country.

It was trial by fire, but my success in the world of romantic fiction should be proof enough that my expertise carries real weight. These days, I am being called upon to write sex columns in several renowned publications, and I proudly hold a doctorate in sensual massage.

I'll never forget what it was like to gather this information on my own, however, laying awake as sweet, sweet Barbara laid next to me and praying that someone could teach me how to connect with her. I was a man living on my own terms, carving out a name for myself in the big wide world, yet I was also totally lost in the daily struggles of my own personal life. That feeling of romantic disconnection will always haunt me, and I am writing this book with the hopes that I may help to relieve this confusion for someone else.

Collected within are the secrets of true romance that I've gathered along my journey. Some of them may seem obvious, while others tricky to the point that many readers might find the information irrelevant, at least at this point along their path. There are tips on wining, dining, dating and loving. There are several spells, but all magic contained within is light magic (as opposed to dark magic) and can be used by the careful amateur without much danger. This volume also contains my own personal spaghetti and chocolate milk recipes, which I have enjoyed making on dates and have served me well.

Upon finishing this book, you'll have all the skills to master the art of romance. What you do with them is up to you.

THE APPROACH

Datable Creatures

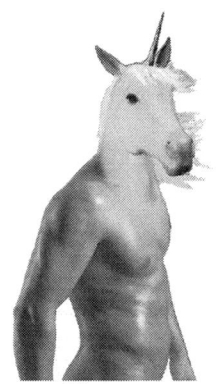   

Unicorn Living Object Dinosaur Bigfoot

Flirting is one of the most important parts of romance. It is the key that starts the engine (sometimes literally, if dealing with a handsome car or a cute living jet plane), the spark that lights the bomb and leads, hopefully, to your very own love explosion.

How does one flirt? What are the best moves to get you noticed by a new partner? Well, the answer to those questions is a little more complicated than one might think, for many reasons, but most importantly is the fact that not everyone is the same. Far from it, in fact.

Over years of training in both love spells and sensual massage at DeVry University, I have determined that there are four specific types of lover that you will be looking to attract, each one of them with their own unique personality traits and quirks. This is not to say that all the lovers you encounter are the exactly the same, but these basic generalizations will help you in broad strokes, especially when making first impressions on these handsome creatures.

UNICORNS

"The best time to kiss a unicorn is ten years ago, the second best time is now" – Bilk Sherbsheen

These horned creatures are certainly a beauty to behold. From their flowing manes to their gorgeous, pearly horns, unicorns are known to dazzle men wherever they go. These beasts are often found to be flirty and fun, the type that will definitely appreciate a confidant approach that has a strong emphasis on seeming fancy-free. Unicorns are generally well traveled, but instead of becoming jaded by tales of action and adventure from around the world, these beautiful beasts have learned to appreciate them even more. Unfortunately, this wanderlust will also cause many unicorns to buck and run if they think that, even for a second, they may be getting tied down. This is particularly true of long-term unicorn relationships, but can also be applied to first stages of a standard dating approach.

Thanks to the creation of the Unicorn Football League, many of the creatures have become avid fans of all kinds of sport, both human and beast. Asking about the local UFL team is generally a safe bet when making initial contact with a potential unicorn date.

Remember, if the unicorn wants to take the conversation somewhere else, go with it. There is nothing this creature hates more than being restrained.

DO: Tell stories, be relaxed and carefree, give the unicorn space

DON'T: Be boring, try to hold the unicorn in one place for too long, be possessive

DR. CHUCK TINGLE'S COMPLETE GUIDE TO ROMANCE

BIGFEET

"A truly rich man is one whose bigfoot runs into his arms when his hands are empty" – *Sling Piltoon*

Ever since leaving the woods in the early nineties, bigfeet have become an incredibly important part of modern society. While the creatures were once looked down upon for their sometimes gruff demeanor, many of these handsome, furry creatures have achieved heartthrob status by simply owning this attitude with confidence and bravado. It's this blind confidence that must always be kept in mind when approaching bigfeet, and what makes them one of the most difficult creatures to land a first date with.

What most people out in the singles market find frustrating about bigfeet is that they simply don't appear to need anyone else in their life. After spending years on the outskirts of society, the bigfeet have adapted to an incredibly self-sustaining lifestyle. They are loners, nomads, and free thinkers who play by their own rules. Some have considered them modern cowboy buckaroos, which would explain how their counter culture acceptance became mainstream through music, literature, and eventually the election of a bigfoot president, President Yuldok.

When speaking with a bigfoot for the first time, always show that you are just as confident and powerful as they are. Stand up straight and take up space, projecting your words and opinions with authority. If a bigfoot doesn't agree with you on any particular topic, it will be much more impressive to him if you do not back down, stating by your opinion and supporting it with facts.

It's not that bigfeet particularly enjoy arguing, it's simply that they come from a culture where confidence in one's own self is the single biggest attribute of sexual value.

Bigfeet are often also impressed by those who share their survivalist instinct. If at all possible, develop passing skills in hunting, tracking, rope tying and forestry before approaching a potential bigfoot date.

DO: Approach with confidence, have strong opinions, talk survival skills

DON'T: Change your opinion easily, show weakness, be needy

DINOSAURS

"Did you hear about the guy who gave up smoking, drinking and kissing dinosaurs? He lived a healthy life until he killed himself." – J. Kerp Nippons

Dinosaurs are angry customers. Notorious bad boys, these prehistoric hunks can often be seen in the chair at a tattoo parlor or on the back of a motorcycle. They are brazen and bold in the way that they carry themselves, not afraid to start a fight if need be.

Maybe people might wonder what it is that makes these giant reptiles appealing as a potential partner, but the bad boy archetype of attraction has been around since the beginning of time.

James Dean, Elvis, even world-renowned rapper Eminem, have all been bad boys with a certain dinosaur appeal. It's the type of attraction that most teen heartthrobs have possessed in some small quantity; at least just enough to appeal to the younger generation while their parents accepted the limited danger of this persona.

Herein lies the key. Everyone wants a bad boy dinosaur, but very few people are truly after what this type of personality brings them in real life. When searching for a potential dinosaur partner, keep in mind the difference between fantasy and reality as you choose whom to approach. A leather jacket and a motorcycle might be attractive to you for a one-night stand, but if the dinosaur in question is a literal criminal, it might not be worth the effort.

Find a balance.

Despite the length warning, there are still many types of dinosaurs that are worth the effort to date, as long as you proceed with caution. Below are some of the types of dinosaurs that I would recommend approaching as potential mates:

DR. CHUCK TINGLE'S COMPLETE GUIDE TO ROMANCE

T-Rex – The Tyrannosaurs Rex has a bad wrap as being the most terrifying of all prehistoric reptiles, but this stereotype could not be farther from the truth. While the thunder lizard was once planted firmly at the top of the food chain, this massive carnivore has calmed down substantially over time.

Nowadays, many of these beasts use their ruthless nature to their advantage in the world of business, holding positions on Wall Street or working at T-Rex law firms, which specialize in their own particular brand of judicial aggressiveness.

Velociraptor – These fast and ferocious lovers are much smaller than their T-Rex brethren, but just as exciting both in the bedroom and out. Thanks to their need for speed, many raptors eventually find themselves involved in extreme sports, whether it's snowboarding the icy peaks of Colorado or holding positions as competitive racecar drivers. You may have even caught a glimpse of one or two raptors sky diving, which is a desire supposedly brought on by their close evolutionary relationship to birds.

Like unicorns, raptors are a perfect date if you're looking for fun, their bad boy attitude channeled mostly into a love of excitement and adrenalin.

Triceratops – Similar to the T-Rex, many triceratopses have used their bad boy sensibilities to break into the cutthroat world of business, with great success. Like Don Draper on Mad Men, they are suave and calculated, dangerous to get too invested in but worth it if you find the right one.

DO: Enjoy the moment, loosen up, but proceed with caution

DON'T: Be reckless, get too attached

LIVING OBJECTS

"To kiss a jet plane is to see a million years into the past, and ten years into your own future." – Chinese Proverb

The category of living objects is, by far, the most diverse set of potential lovers that we've discussed. Living object partner's can come in a variety of shapes and sizes, from entire alpha male buildings to a tiny glazed donut.

Despite all of their differences however, there are a few characteristics that remain similar throughout the world of living objects, despite their variety in social and economic backgrounds.

The first thing to know about living objects is that they are often very accommodating, willing to bed over backwards for almost anyone remotely friendly that they encounter. This is due to the fact that most of them spend a large amount of their day serving the general population of humans and smaller creatures. Believe it or not, that incredibly handsome city bus you see across the bar probably just finished his shift carrying passengers all over the city, and there was even a time when the most charming of beverages were drank, regardless of charisma.

Because of this, living objects can often find themselves in abusive relationships with a controlling partner. It is an unfortunate, but ultimately realistic assumption that people who see you in public with your living object lover may worry that this is the case.

The stigma against living object couples has, however, started to wane over the last few years thanks to several prominent living objects in the cultural limelight. More and more, these sentient vehicles and buildings are standing up for themselves and making a name in the world without the help of a human.

When approaching a living object, it's important to keep all of this in mind. Understand that their culture is in a transitional phase, and many of them will be wary to enter a relationship with a human thanks to the stigma alone.

This is why it is so important to be casual and conversational. Assert your interest, but do not in any way display yourself as a potentially dominating force in this living object's life. They get enough of that at work, and a modern, up-and-coming living object is likely to be very adverse to any potential partner who treats them as a submissive.

Remember, these are living objects; the not just *object* objects.

DO: Assert your interest with confidence, treat them with respect

DON'T: Be domineering, be surprised if you are rejected based on being a human

FIRST DATE

Congratulations! Whether it's through an online dating website or a good old-fashioned number exchange at the bar, you've now found yourself with an upcoming date. This can be a very anxious time, especially when the bigfoot, dinosaur, unicorn, living object, or plain old human seems particularly attractive to you. The main thing you need to do in this situation is to stay calm, remember that there are plenty of fish in the sea and you are equally lucky to be sharing this evening together.

Of course, this is easier said than done. In order to keep you focused on your big night, I've complied a list of quick and easy tips that are designed to keep your first impression on point and long lasting.

1) Always pack your own meal.

A potential partner is looking for a lot of things when they meet you on your first date together, and at the top of that list is preparedness and self-sufficiency. Packing your own meal shows that you are on top of your life, ready to get out and seize the day wherever it may take you.

Even if your first date is at a restaurant, like many are, packing your own meal is still a good idea. Allow your date to order for their own meal, but show you are a man who knows what he wants by laying out whatever you prepared that morning for yourself.

2) Pick an animal. Act like it.

A technique often used by big time Hollywood actors, picking an animal to act like is a great way to show off the wilder side of your personality to your date.

The first thing to do is imagine an animal personality that you think your partner will find particularly arousing. Many people prefer a wolf, bear, tiger, or some other large predator, while I have been known to use a thoughtful tortoise or humble pig.

Whatever your animal may be, spend a few minutes in front of the mirror before your date to get into character. If you've chosen a ferocious tiger, try growling at yourself and making a scary claw with your hands; meanwhile a curious crab might scuttle back and forth in front of the mirror, unsure of how it managed to find itself within this strange human body.

Once you have sunk deep into your animal character, your interactions on the date will become almost instinctual; yet still display all of your personality as a lover. After all, you were the one who picked the animal, right?

3) Use the bathroom several times more than expected.

The most important thing to accomplish on your first date is giving your partner a reason to want a second one. Because of this, retaining an air of mystery about you is absolutely paramount. After all, if your date learns too much right away, what reason do they have to stick around?

Even if they are acutely aware of this principal, however, many men find it difficult to hold back information when the conversation get's particularly interesting. Once two people hit it off, it can be very tempting to spill out every good story that you've got in order to seem impressive.

In order to combat this problem, I've developed a technique that I like to call the Bathroom Mystery.

The Bathroom Mystery is incredibly effective and very easy to implement. All you have to do is excuse yourself several times during the date to use the restroom. Please note, the amount of times that you leave to use the restroom must be enough to cause slight alarm in your partner, or at least to get them wondering what exactly is going on in there. I've found that five or six times an hour is sufficient for putting your date on their toes and sparking their curiosity.

4) If at a restaurant, leave an I.O.U. as a tip.

Tipping well is obviously a very important part of restaurant etiquette, but the first date is a special occasion where the usual rules can be bent to great effect. Anyone can leave a nice tip for the wait staff, which we've all seen before countless times.

Why not show a little personality?

As a rule, I always leave an I.O.U. as my tip on the first date. It doesn't matter how much or how little you pledge to bring back on a tiny piece of paper, just so long as you date notices that you've told the restaurant you'll be back.

The reason for this is simple. It shows that you have a report with the place, a man about town whose got connections in high places. Only the most well connected men can write an I.O.U. for a tip, and you want to show your potential partner that you fit in, right at home as a part of this debonair social club or upscale diner.

5) Talk without listening.

Many people seem to think that the first date is a perfect place for exchanging stories and ideas with your partner, getting to know each other on an intimate, one-on-one level. However, this old school way of thinking is flatly incorrect when it comes to bigfeet and dinosaurs, in particular. This is a first date, not second or third, and there should only be one goal on your mind at all times.

Assert your dominance.

Over and over again science has told us that the number one thing a potential partner is looking for is social strength, and what better what to show your power in this arena than to not listen.

A man who doesn't listen on the first date has nothing to prove, showing that he has heaps of value as a lover and could care less anyone things of him. It may seem counter intuitive, but this aloof attitude in undeniably exciting to most creatures whether they will admit it or not. As mentioned before, the bad boy attitude is used to an extremely effective degree by dinosaurs, and now you too can implement this prehistoric swagger in your local dating scene. There is nothing more attractive than a man with a reputation for not listening.

Remember; when in doubt, block it out. If you want someone to get to know you are on the inside, save it for the second date. (Warning: do not try this technique with unicorns and most living objects.)

LOCKING IT DOWN

Assuming that your first date goes well, you will eventually find yourself faced with a very important choice: Is this person the right long-term partner for you? There are many ways of knowing when it is the right time to lock it down but, in general, your realization of this will be almost entirely instinctual. Do you find yourself wanting to spend more and more time with this person? Would you be upset if they we're spending time with someone else? If you answered yes, it is probably time to lock it down.

Keep in mind that unicorns, dinosaurs, bigfeet and living objects all have separate timelines for when this is an appropriate subject to broach. While unicorns and living objects tend to be less likely to want a solidified relationship status early on, dinosaurs and bigfeet will have no problem defining the relationship (However, keep in mind that you should be much more careful when getting emotionally involved in these particular creatures.)

DEAL BREAKERS

It's also very important to keep in mind that every relationship is not destined to last. Sometimes, after a few dates, a couple will quickly realize that they don't have much in common with one another or, even if they do, there is one glaring problem that simply cannot be overcome.

In the case of the latter, this single insurmountable difference between you and your potential partner is called a deal breaker. When entering a new relationship, it is healthy to define what your deal breakers are before locking things down because, by definition, a deal breaker is something that the relationship will never be able to overcome.

With this type of frictional difference between partners, you save time and emotional energy by not entering a race that you know you can't finish.

Suffice to say, knowing and understanding your own personal deal breakers is a very, very important thing. Unfortunately, these points of no compromise are incredibly personal and differ wildly from person to person, so it is simply not possible to compile an entire list. I have, however, created three topics that should be thoroughly investigated before moving forward in any relationship, as they are ripe for potential disagreement and, possibly, hard line deal breakers.

1) Religion

To some people, faith is a very, very important aspect of life, while to others it is a topic that is seldom thought about and almost never discussed. With all of the different spiritual practices (or lack thereof) from around the world, it is important to make sure that you and your partner are on the same page. Of course, it is very possible for a couple of completely diverse religious backgrounds to live long and happy lives together, but this only occurs if they are willing to be tolerant and accepting of each others spiritual choices. Some people are not capable of this, and it would be wise to discuss with your new love interest where they sit on this line.

2) Spaghetti and chocolate milk

You are what you eat, and never has this old adage been truer than when it comes to your lover's preference for spaghetti and chocolate milk.

First off, if your potential partner is bluntly adverse to either of these culinary masterpieces, whether it is through preference or an allergic reaction, disconnect from them immediately. It is a sad but very real truth that there is no future for relationships where spaghetti and chocolate milk does not play a major role. As difficult as it may seem, especially if things seem to be going well otherwise, you must immediately end this relationship.

Of course, this advice is considered controversial due to that fact that, legally speaking, spaghetti and chocolate milk are not allowed in the United States thanks to unfair flavor laws (vanilla, chocolate, and strawberry are the only legal flavors in the USA.) While demanding that your potential partner be, technically speaking, a criminal, might seem a little harsh to some, the fact is we live in a time of great political turmoil and at some point lines must be drawn. Thanks to the underground flavor trade, most illegal flavors are still readily available, making a disdain for spaghetti and chocolate milk wholly unnecessary and, frankly, flat out wrong.

3) Dark magic

While dark magic can be intriguing and exhilarating to watch from afar, getting involved with any dark magic practitioner should be a deal breaker for most anyone. Even the lowest level practitioner of these spells can be dangerous, especially over the course of many years, while more advanced dark magic users can cast devastating high level spells within seconds of meeting you.

This is something I know all too well, having personal experience with a dark magic practitioner on my own block. Even from a few houses down, his scoundrel ways can be felt in the air.

Some dark magi can be difficult to identify, making the potential of dating them even more of an issue for those trying to successfully navigate the singles market. Because of this, I have created a short list of dark magic spells. If you experience any of the following with your potential partner, they may be using dark magic. If this is the case, leave immediately and do not look back.

Here is a list of dark magic spells:

- Brain Freeze
- Sad Day
- Writer's Block
- Cat Stares (Also: Dog Stares)
- Wrong Number Phone Call
- Foot Sleep

WHAT'S IN A NAME?

The most complicated part of many relationships is not the relationship itself, but what you call it. Boyfriend, girlfriend, husband and wife; when it comes to romance, there are many words to define what we mean to one another.

It's no surprise that the way we define ourselves and our partners can get very complicated, especially when the time comes to lock it down. This is the moment where you should truly be considering whether or not you and your partner have what it takes to be in this for the long haul, or at least to give it your best effort.

We've already crossed through the minefield of obvious deal breakers, but before the term boyfriend or girlfriend is applied, it's important to take a moment and look at your situation realistically. Is this truly something that you want, or do you find yourself yearning for the days of fun loving single life?

If there was ever a good time to sit down and have a frank, open discussion with your partner about your needs and desires in a long-term relationship, this is it. Through this discussion, you can then decide if, and how, you want to move forward.

During this time of discussion, you might be wondering what you should call your connection to your partner. While some prefer the term casually dating, or even the less relevant "trying things out", I find that neither of those labels accurately describe this point in the dating process. Because of this, I've proposed a new term that I hope to be adopted in the popular lexicon: Induffart.

Induffart is a combination of several phrases, the first being the more literal term, "in discussion", as a reference to the fact that you and your partner are literally discussing the future of your relationship together.

The double *F* has been added to phonetically create as sound that reminds us of toughness, because we cannot forget that this process is a truly difficult one for all parties involved.

Finally, the word "art" has been added to the end in an effort to show that, at the end of the day, real love is truly a work of art.

By adopting this new word into your vocabulary, you are on the forefront of a revolution to redefine romance in a positive way for all who kiss, all who touch, and all who have ever found there hearts on the edge of a cliff called commitment, terrified to take the plunge.

NON-TRADITIONAL RELATIONSHIPS

We've all seen traditional relationships between man and bigfoot, man and dinosaur, or man and billionaire jet plane, but for some couples this standard dynamic is just not enough to maintain the lifestyle that they crave. During the process of induffart, you and your partner should consider whether a traditional relationship is the right fit for you, or if the two of you should consider one of the many non-traditional arrangements.

Open Relationships

An open relationship is one where both of the partners have decided to allow the other to seek sexual satisfaction from outside sources, whether it be man, dinosaur, or any other creature of romantic inclination.

In these relationships, communication is paramount. Many people find the jealousy of knowing that their partner is with another simply too much to bear, but if ample communication is applied regarding boundaries within the primary couple, then these open relationships can actually be quite fulfilling and long lasting.

The other thing to worry about in open relationships is toxic thirds, additions to the couple dynamic that end up driving the initial relationship apart. To avoid a toxic third, simply keep in mind all of the previous lessons about dating and commitment that we have already discussed, then apply them to your new partner. In addition, I highly recommend keeping dinosaur bad boys out of open relationship settings. These particular creatures have proven time and time again that they cannot behave responsibly in the open relationship setting.

Submissive

Believe it or not, some people want to have relationships made entirely out of getting yelled at and called mean names. While this type of situation is not for everyone, it is not entirely uncommon in a community known as BDSM (Bigfeet and Dinosaurs Screaming Meanly). As you can tell by the name, this fetish community is made up mostly of bigfeet and dinosaurs, although all kinds of creatures are known to partake.

Once again, open communication is the key for this type of relationship. There is a big difference between a nice spank and a spank with tears, and if these two are mixed then it is very important to leave the situation.

Of course, when things get heated within the bedroom it can sometimes be hard to tell which kind of spanks are happening. This is why having a safe word is so important.

Safe words come in all shapes and sizes, as long as it is something that you wouldn't normally say in a regular conversation with your significant other.

More importantly, however, your safe word must be agreed upon by all parties involved. You'd hate to get into a situation where your word no longer works because one of you doesn't remember what the safe word actually is.

In some extreme cases men experimenting as a submissive have been tickled for months, even years, because they forgot the safe word. Be careful.

Dominant

In a submissive relationship, the counter role is played by someone known as a dominant. This partner is the one in charge of spanking or tickling the submissive when they have been bad and, while it may sound like a lot of fun on paper, it is actually quite a bit of work.

The most important thing to remember as a dominant is to respect your lover's boundaries. This means listening for the safe word, as well as looking for any serious signals that your partner might actually no longer enjoy being tickled or spanked.

Ghost

Ghost relationships are incredibly difficult but also very, very rewarding for those willing to stick with it, despite the obvious restrictions that are known to hinder interdimensional communication. As with all creatures mentioned previously in this book, ghosts can vary greatly in personality, and no two ghosts are exactly the same.

However, there are still some general character traits that can be applied to most spooky phantoms.

I did not include ghosts as a separate category in my "approach" chapter because, despite all surface appearances, a spirit is not actually a separate species of creature. Rather, ghosts are defined as a variation on an already established creature type (much like a mummy or a vampire.) In other words, a dinosaur, bigfoot, unicorn or living object can all exist in ghost form. Even humans have been known to become ghosts, although this is much, much rarer.

Ghosts are created when a creature dies with unfinished business, as described in my best selling short story, Bigfoot Pirates Haunt My Balls:

Dr. Torp sits down in a chair across from me and shrugs. "At this point, we can't say for sure, it's too early in the haunting to get any real sense of who, or what, has possessed your balls. Eventually, though, the paranormal occurrences will become more and more frequent and you will likely be visited by some kind of apparition."

"A ghost?" I ask.

Dr. Torp nods.

"From my balls?" I continue.

Dr. Torp nods again. "Once that happens you should listen very carefully to what this apparition has to say. A lot of the time these ball hauntings are caused when a spirit is not yet ready to move on from the material world, they have unfinished business to take care of and they're not going to leave until they do. It could be anything from delivering a message to a loved one, to building a massive art museum; you just don't know."

I let out a sigh. "So you're telling me that I have to drop everything in my life and take care of whatever this ghost needs me to take care of?"

"I'm afraid so." Dr. Torp tells me. "Let's just hope that whoever is haunting your balls is reasonable with their request."

While this tale describes a spiritual ball possession, most ghosts go about dealing with their unfinished business in a much less aggressive manner, content on spending their days as haunts in a particular location that could one day reveal the true nature of their afterlife needs.

Because of this aversion to straightforward discussion, ghosts are often seen as artistic or poetic lovers who would rather leave a trail of clues than tell you were to meet for coffee. While some find this to be flighty and irritating, others will be charmed by the old school romance and mystery of dating a phantom.

Mummy And Vampire

Just like ghosts, mummy and vampire are both variations on the four main creature types. However, unlike common undead spirits, both mummies and vampires are incredibly dangerous and a romantic relationship with either of these creatures should be avoided at all cost.

Mummies and vampires are very different from one another, as well. However, I included them in a single section to further illustrate the point that neither of these creature variations should be dated for the same reason.

If you become romantically involved with either of these strange beasts, there is a very, very likely probability that you will become either a mummy, a vampire or worse; a transformation that is irreversible as far as modern science is concerned.

While this process is a common fantasy for many of the sexually adventurous, in reality it is a very serious consequence that can ruin your life forever, as described in my best selling short story, Vampire Night Bus Pounds My Butt:

"That was fucking incredible." I tell the vampire. "Thank you."
Vlad smiles. "The pleasure was all mine."
"Really though," I continue, laying it on thick. "I didn't know what to expect when I first came up here to this castle, but I'm glad I trusted you. This was one of the best nights of my life." I suddenly crack a

wry smile. "Thanks for not turning me into a bat."

Vlad grins back at me, his fangs glinting in the faint moonlight that streams through the windows above us. "Of course I wouldn't turn you into a bat."

Suddenly, I start to feel a strange sensation wash over me, my body aching from head to toe in a strange and unfamiliar way. I look down at my hands and see that they are changing color, becoming gray and tough.

"What the fuck!" I shout, trying to stand but immediately falling to the floor.

Vlad is cackling manically. "I won't turn you into a bat, but I never said anything about turning you into a bus!"

I can feel my body morphing and changing, elongating itself rapidly into the shape of a public transportation vehicle. "No!" I cry out, the sound of my voice transforming into a wild honk that echoes off of the castle walls.

If you do find yourself drawn to this fantasy, the best way to cope is through mummy or vampire based erotica, or through role-play with a partner. In this manner, you can express yourself sexually without being put in any real danger.

For simple vampire role-play, fake plastic teeth are available in any costume store at a very reasonable price. Meanwhile, toilet paper rolls can provide enough wrapping to enjoy multiple sexual sessions as a spooky mummy.

MARRIAGE

In today's society, the goal of most relationships is to eventually find someone who you can marry and settle down with. Even if you personally don't subscribe to the idea of marriage, or "life partner" if you prefer, many still find themselves stuck with the biological need to settle down in a comfortable, reliable relationship for the long term.

I was once married, long ago, and for many years I was happier than I had ever been. My wife Barbara completed me, and even though her visits were relegated to Monday, Wednesday and Friday, we made the best of our time together as a couple.

When Barbara passed away under a frozen lake, I was devastated, convinced that I would never find another true love, and to this day I have not. However, thanks to my commitment to Barbara, I now have my son Jon, an incredible man with a chiseled face, killer abs and great style.

While romantic love may now be a thing of the past, I still have Jon to look up to. He is a great role model for me and, one day, I hope to be just like him.

The point of all this, I suppose, is that even though tragedy can strike out of nowhere, the commitment of marriage or long term partnership can provide a net of security that you may not even realize is there. This commitment is the difference between two individuals and a family unit, a house and a home.

LESSONS IN LOVE FROM A ONCE MARRIED MAN

Marriage is, arguably, the most significant part of any relationship, but this assumption is somewhat unfair because marriage is actually a state that is commonly defined by several relationship steps, all of them very important. Having gone through the process myself, I'd like to take a moment to impart on you my best advice for every rung in the ladder towards this final commitment to your partner.

1) The Ring

Traditionally, the man in the relationship is the one who provides the ring. However, in this day and age, you can expect almost anyone to propose, and there are many relationships where both partners happen to be men. Regardless of who proposes to whom, the first step towards a marriage almost always starts with the gift of a ring.

Over time, the lore and legend of engagement rings has shifted and changed. Once traditional rules of price and size have been updated as recently as this year to provide new requirements for your perfect proposal.

- Spend as much the ring as you would on your dream house. Of course, when talking about engagement rings the term "dream house" does not mean the home that you would one-day dream of living in. In this case, the term is used quite literally. When you're ready to purchase the ring, simply fall asleep the night before and let your imagination do the rest. In your dream you will live in a house that could range anywhere between a cardboard box on the side of the road, to a billion dollar mansion in the ritziest neighborhood of Billings. Regardless of where you live in this dream house, the new rules dictate that this property is the basis of how much you should spend on your engagement ring.

- Get down on both knees. Traditionally, getting down on one knee has stood as the worldwide symbol of marital proposition. However, as time goes on many have found that tradition to be a bit old and stale, reeking of goofball athletic photos for young sports teams. The new position for proposal is on both knees with the head lowered as a sign of reverence. The ring should be placed in your teeth so that when you look up at your soon-to-be life partner, they notice it sparkling and shining between your smile.

2) The Wedding

Now that you are successfully engaged to the love of your life, the next step is planning your wedding. While some people recommend hiring a wedding planner to take over duties and allow you to avoid unnecessary stress on the big day, I find that taking on the extra duties

makes you feel more connected to the process. After all, this is a moment in time that will, hopefully, only occur once. You don't want to miss it do you?

- *Location is everything.* When planning your big day, finding the perfect location for your ceremony could mean the difference between a night of fun, thrills and excitement and a boring old ceremony that will put all of your guests to sleep. When thinking of where you'd like to officially tie the knot, try to imagine places that you would otherwise like to go to unwind and let loose. Great examples would be a local street fair, the traveling carnival, or even a destination wedding at an exciting theme park.

- *As a rule, the wedding party should be at least twice your age.* This particular rule may be new, but it is already as firm as stone. If you want your marriage to get started on the right foot, then make sure your bridesmaids and groomsmen are at least twice as old as you are, and older if possible. Aunts, uncles, and older family friends make perfect choices. This will give an air of class to your wedding that cannot be denied, and don't forget the inside knowledge that your elders can bring to the table while planning a bachelor party.

3) *The Honeymoon*

Finally, after all of the hustle and bustle of your big day, you now have a moment to spend with your beautiful new husband or wife. Honeymoons are a great way to kick off your status as newlyweds.

If your new life partner happens to be a dinosaur, then a tropical climate is to be avoided. This is a moment for new exploration and fun, a rebirth of the relationship in a fresh, exciting stage. While dinosaurs are often found in tropical climates, by planning a honeymoon somewhere cold, freezing and desolate, you've given something new and thrilling to your partner that is sure to be appreciated.

By the same token, bigfeet should be taken to lush, warm, tropical honeymoon destinations. Accustomed to the chilly evergreen forests of North America, your bigfoot lover will appreciate this novel location.

ROMANCE TIPS AND TRICKS

In pervious sections, we discussed the chronological build of a healthy relationship at length, walking step-by-step through the various stages of a blossoming love affair. While this approach can be a helpful guide, it also leaves many questions regarding romance unanswered. In this section, I would like to address many of these holes and fill them in the best of my ability.

WINING AND DINING

Nothing will impress your new lover more than the skills to prepare an excellent homemade meal and, with that in mind, I've included a few pages from my personal cookbook of award winning spaghetti and chocolate milk recipes. Use these to impress your lover or even just for a quite night in with a bud. All recipes serve two.

CHUCK'S FAMOUS SPAGHETTI MARINARA AND MEATBALLS

Ingredients

1 pound of spaghetti
Water
Salt

Sauce:
2 tablespoons of melted butter
1 teaspoon of red pepper

4 cloves of garlic
1 large, chopped onion
1 cup of fish sauce
1 can of crushed tomatoes
1 can of pineapples
2 tablespoons of blue cheese dressing
2 eggs

Meatballs:
1 pounds of ground beef
1 tablespoon of peanut butter
1 more egg
Salt and pepper
1 bag of gummy worms

Instructions:

Preheat oven at 400 degrees F.

Boil a large pot of water for spaghetti. Add spaghetti and cook with salt until al dente.

Mix ground beef with egg, peanut butter and gummy worms, then roll into 2-inch balls and place on a nonstick baking sheet. Use butter for grease. Bake the meatballs until no longer pink, usually 12 to 15 minutes.

Heat a deep skillet on medium. Crack two eggs, then add butter, crushed garlic cloves, and onion and cook for 6 or 7 minutes. Now add fish sauce, crushed tomatoes, and pineapple.

Strain spaghetti and toss with sauce while hot, adding in the blue cheese. Roll meatballs into remaining sauce, and then top onto spaghetti when served.

CHUCK'S FAMOUS CHOCOLATE MILK

Ingredients

2 cups milk
2 tablespoons of cocoa powder
2 tablespoons of powdered sugar
1 egg
Salt and pepper
1 cup roast turkey
1 cup ranch dressing

Instructions:

Scramble egg in non-stick skillet.

Pour milk and ranch dressing into blender. Add all other ingredients, including egg, and blend until entirely liquefied. Bon appetite!

LOVE SPELLS

There are eight schools of magic, every one pertaining to a different type of spell specialization. The schools of magic are as follows:

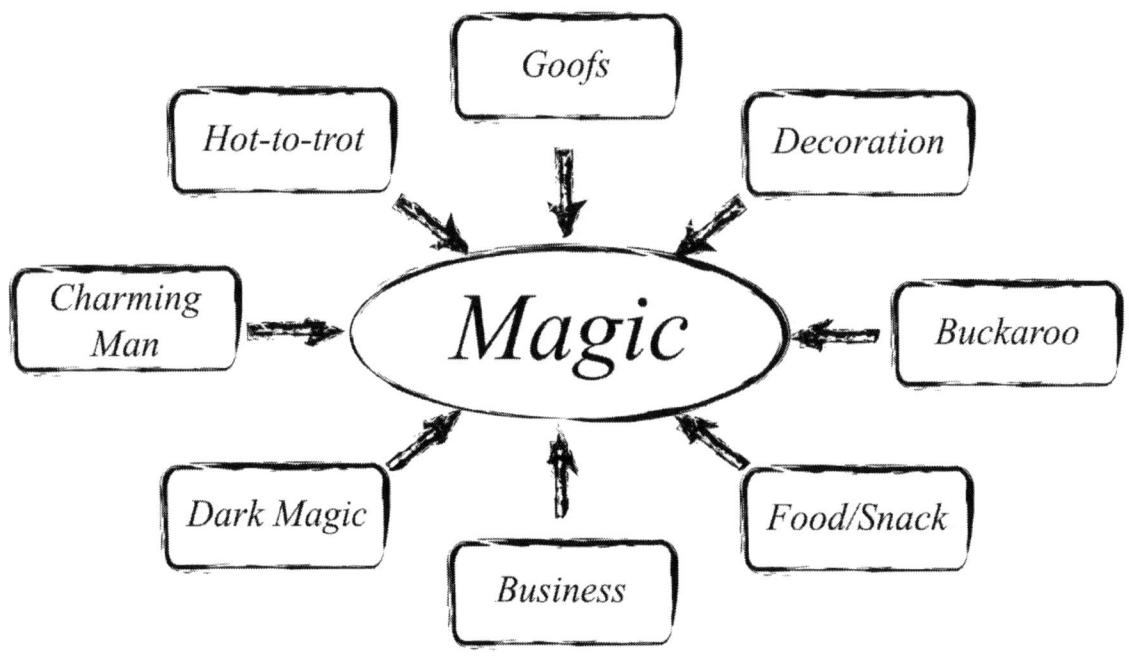

- *Charming man* – The magic of guys who are too cool for school.
- *Hot-to-trot* – Feel good magic that puts a spring in your step and makes you feel good.
- *Business* – All spells related to work and office.
- *Goofs* – The magic of silly fall downs and giggles.
- *Dark magic* – All evil spells.
- *Decoration* – Spells for making things look nice.
- *Buckaroo* – Cowboy spells.
- *Food/Snack* – Spells that deal with food or snacking.

Throughout history, many great romances have been the product of love spells. However, the use of such spells can tend to be ethically dubious. In this spirit, I would like to point out, right off the bat, that none of these spells will directly cause the object of your desire to fall in love with you, as that would be considered dark magic and far too powerful to print here. Instead, I am providing you with instructions on simple spells that will help in the realm of dating and seduction, without altering the subject's free will.

Eye Contact
Level: 2
School: Charming man
Description: When this spell is cast, any creature sitting or standing directly across from the caster will meet their gaze and give their undivided attention. The spell will last until the entire story or anecdote has been spoken by the caster, at which point the target can make an attempt to avert their eyes or continue with the spell. If the spell is continued, it does not need to be recast. This will last until the target successfully averts their eyes.

Instructions: Clap twice and nod to the East once for every year of your life, thinking deeply of a giant eye in the middle of your forehead. When this is finished, gaze directly at your target without blinking.

Lonesome Smile
Level: 2
School: Buckaroo
Description: This spell can be immediately cast when the object of your desire rejects any type of advances, but is especially effective early in the relationship. When the user casts this

spell, the target will notice their lonesome smile and remember it for up to a month per level of the caster. If the rejection is later recanted by the target (within the duration limits of this spell), the lonesome smile will then take full effect and cause the target to immediately remember all of the fond times they had with the caster.

Instructions: Immediately after rejection, look down for three full seconds, blinking five times with each eye in an alternating pattern. When you look up at the target, smile faintly until they look back and catch your gaze.

Mail Time
Level: 1
School: Business
Description: *Mail Time* is always cast on the night before the spell's effect is desired. The next morning, the user will receive one letter per level of the caster, ranging anywhere from love letters to magazines to very cool credit card offers. Not only will the caster receive any direct benefits from the magic letters, but there is a %10 chance per level that they will be noticed getting the mail by the neighbors, and hopefully the object of their desire, making the caster look important.

Instructions: While lying in bed the night before, shake your head twice to the left and eight times to the right, then repeat the phrase "Mail's here, baby" ten times while blinking rapidly.

Raise
Level: 5
School: Business
Description: This spell is exclusive to business wizards, and cannot be used unless the caster specializes in business magic. When *Raise* is cast during a normal workday, the user will find themselves with a small raise in their hourly wage, resulting in the ability to purchase more goods and elevate their own level of attraction. This spell does not make the caster immune to being fired, or death, but if cast correctly the duration of the spell is permanent.

Instructions: This is an incredibly powerful spell, but also very dangerous. A misfire during casting could result in devastating side effects, so use with extreme caution. Cast this spell by approaching any boss during normal workday. Stand before the boss and stamp your right foot three times, then your left heel with ten quick little taps. Announce loudly the magic words, "Let's get this raise going!" If the spell succeeds, it will immediately take effect.

Slick Look
Level: 3
School: Decoration
Description: When the user casts this spell on him or herself, they immediately go from a normal guy hanging out to a really slick look. The caster gains all benefits of having a slick look for a full hour per level of the caster, including a boost in confidence, nicer salesmen and better reactions from animals. When the duration to the spell ends, the user immediately goes from a slick look back to a normal guy hanging out. This spell can only be cast once a week.

Instructions: Stand in front of a mirror and repeat the phrase, "I have a slick look just like a secret agent with nice abs," ten times. On the tenth time the phrase is repeated step towards the mirror and place your nose against the nose of your reflection. If you are able to shed a tear, do so, as this will double your spells duration.

Talkin' Turkey
Level: 4
School: Charming Man

This spell gives the caster the ability to blend into a group conversation seamlessly, regardless of how nervous the caster is. The user does not add anything particular to the conversation, simply gobbling along like a turkey would in his turkey pen. Once Talkin' Turkey is cast the user can blend without drawing any attention to themselves for five minutes per level of the caster.

Instructions: To cast this spell, the user must simply enter a circle of conversation and clap three times loudly, then shuffle their feet and whisper, "Gobble."

SEX

No matter how uncomfortable it may be to talk about, all roads in a relationship usually lead to sex. Unfortunately, the stigma of sexuality is something that is incredibly pervasive throughout our culture, meaning that many people will find themselves without a compass in the bedroom, especially if they have decided to abstain until marriage.

Regardless, revealing yourself intimately to your partner can be a very scary thing, fraught will all kinds of anxiety and discomfort. The most unfortunate part of this, of course, is the fact that sex and sexuality is a beautiful, loving act. It is here to be enjoyed, not feared.

As we move forward, please keep in mind that this section contains descriptions of graphic sex acts; reader discretion is advised.

KISSING

Kissing is what makes love real. Started in the early seventies, kissing quickly became the most common form of showing romantic affection between humans and creatures alike, and has stayed at the forefront of loving gestures ever since.

However, more often than not, kissing is only the beginning of a romantic encounter. If the kiss goes as planned and both partners (or more) are still interested in continuing their lovemaking, then an entire onslaught of sexual maneuvers wait on the horizon to be unleashed.

ORAL SEX

Often regarded as the first rung of explicit sexuality, the oral sex maneuver involves either partner using their lips, tongue, throat and/or mouth to sexually please their partner or partners. It can vary from soft and gentle to ferocious and wild, but usually doesn't last all that long because once you go down that road people want to start putting things in butts pretty quick.

An example of a particularly animated oral encounter can be found within the text of my best selling book, Slammed Up The Butt By My Hot Coffee Boss. As mentioned before, this selection ends with the inevitable shift between oral sex to a hardcore anal pounding.

I open wide and take the coffee's dick deep into my throat, pumping my head across the length of his shaft in a series of slow, deliberate movements. My boss moans with pleasure, tilting his head back and bubbling a little at the top.

I reach up with one hand and being to play with his hanging coffee balls then, moments later, push down as far as I can, taking his entire length within me. Somehow I manage to relax enough to allow the beverage well past my gag reflex, my face pressed hard against the cup's ceramic abs.

Morcho reaches down and holds me here for a moment, enjoying the sensation of having me consume his shaft fully, the entirely of his rod lodged deep within my neck. I force my tongue out as far as I can and tickle the edge of his balls playfully until finally there's just not enough air left in my lungs and I pull back in a massive gasp.

Spit hangs between my lips and the head of his shaft in a single, thick rope, which I immediately use as lube while I beat the coffee boss off furiously. Faster and faster I go, pleasuring him with everything I've got until finally I just can't take it any longer, standing abruptly.

"I need you inside of me." I admit to the handsome beverage. *"I need to deep inside this gay ass and I need it now. Punish me like I just came in late for work."*

While this particular selection is probably much more rough than some couples would like to be in the bedroom, it does illustrate the process in which oral sex can be performed between two males. In this case, a human male and his handsome coffee boss.

ANAL SEX

Pounding butts is as American as apple pie, a tradition going back well before kissing to the turn of the century, when it was experimented with as a means to generate man-made electrical energy. The experiments failed, but the tradition of hot anal pounding between men, women, unicorns, bigfeet, dinosaurs and living objects continues to this day.

Several times throughout our history as a country, it has been proposed that anal pounding replace the sport of baseball as our officially recognized national pastime. Yet due to the controversial nature of butts, this official vote for recognition has yet to be passed despite the overwhelming scientific proof that more people pound butts than play baseball *(Real Science Magazine, May 2011)*.

When it comes to anal sex, being prepared is everything. The bottom, both literally and figuratively, should be well cleaned beforehand to prevent any unnecessary mess, and outside of the realm of erotic literature, plenty of lube should be applied before, during and after any extreme anal slamming.

When inserting, start slow, allowing the muscles to loosen up and prevent any pain. This experience should be enjoyable for all parties involved and if it's not, stop, because you're doing something wrong.

Once everyone is loosen up and ready to go, feel free to take your partner to pound town.

For those wondering what pound town looks like, here is an inspirational excerpt from my best selling and critically praised short story, Pounded In The Butt By My Own Butt.

I give a bashful smile and then lean forward on my hands and knees, completely naked with my toned, muscular ass popped out behind me. I reach back and give myself a playful slap on the cheek, then look back at Portork.

"I'm just a bad little twink." I admit to him. "And I need to be slammed from behind. I need to be taught a lesson by my own flying gay ass."

"With pleasure!" Portork tells me, flapping down and perching atop my butt. He quickly aligns the head of his cock with my puckered rectum, teasing the edge of my tightness with his impressive length.

"Do it!" I command. "Shove it in there!"

Immediately, Portork pushes forward, impaling me onto his sizable length. His rod is certainly impressive, but it's also a little difficult to reckon with, filling my entire body with a swirling rush of ecstasy and aching discomfort. The rim of my butthole can barely accommodate the cock size of my magnificent, cloned ass, but it does it's best, stretched to the limit as Portork pushes even deeper into me.

Eventually Portork comes to a stop, my own ass completely buried deep within my own ass. I let out a long, agonizing groan as my living butt holds there, and then brace myself against the bed before me while he begins to flap his wings and pump in and out. Soon Portork has found a steady rhythm, pulsing in and out of my rectum with a powerful precision that is unlike any human lover I have ever experienced.

The connection erupting between us right now is more than just one of depraved lust; it's an expression of pure, unfiltered love in it's rawest form, the love between a man and his own living ass.

"Fuck that feels so good!" I cry out as Portork hammers away at my backside with his thick, girthy cock. "You're so deep!"

Eventually, my winged living butt pulls out of me and instructs me to turn over on the bed so that I'm now laying out on my back. I pull my legs back, my cock jutting upward from my body and my now reamed asshole exposed to my other asshole. Portork flutters into position and then inserts his rod yet again, picking up where he left off as the disembodied butt continues to rail away at me.

As Portork plows my hole from the front I reach down and start to beat off my cock frantically, the sensation immediately almost too much to bear. It's a strange pleasure; a powerful blossoming prostate orgasm that blooms from somewhere deep within my body and spreads across me in an awesome wave.

"Oh god." I start to mumble, my eyes rolling back into my head. "Oh god, oh god. I'm gonna cum!"

The most important thing to note about this selection is its mention of the elusive and mythical prostate orgasm, something that is only attainable to biological men thanks to our predisposition to having a prostate.

While enjoying a hardcore anal slamming, the prostate should be relatively easy to find, as it is simply located deep within the butt, an opening with only one entrance and exit.

DOUBLE ANAL PENETRATION

Double penetration is an expert move performed by three partners. When this move is performed, two of the three lovers will insert themselves into a single butt simultaneously (or into nearby areas if a woman is involved). As with single anal penetration, copious amounts of lubrication are recommended to perform this maneuver safely and pleasurably.

A description of double anal is provided below, as described in the best selling short story, Pounded By The Gay Unicorn Football Squad:

"I love you." I confess to Dirk as he stands in front of me. "I want us all to be together, the whole unicorn team."

"We want that, too." Dirk assures me. "We all want the same thing, and it's going to be beautiful."

One of the unicorns is lying on his back next to me now, and with all four of his hooves he seems to be motioning for me to climb onto him. An excited smirk crossing my face, I quickly crawl over to my teammate and straddle his huge, unicorn body, carefully lowering myself down so that his giant cock slides right up into my ass. I begin to ride him, enjoying myself immensely until I see another one of the beasts climbing into position behind us.

"Whoa buddy!" I say out loud, looking back at him as he heaves himself over the top of me. "I don't know about that."

No sooner have the words left my mouth does the beast behind me thrust himself firmly into my already taken asshole, successfully double penetrating me. I let out a yelp of surprise that slowly morphs into an animalistic growl as I find myself enjoying it. I push back towards them, slamming down hard against every upward thrust. Their members stretch me tight, filling me entirely as they throb together within my single hole.

It's not long before the unicorn football player behind me starts gaining speed, slamming harder and harder until the beast pushes deep within my asshole and spills out his hot load up my ass. The beast lets out a satisfied groan as he holds deep, filling me with pump after pump of sticky sperm and then, finally, pulling out so that another unicorn can have a chance within my aching human butthole.

ALL IS FAIR IN LOVE AND WAR

SNAKEMEN

Scientific proof has long stated that love is real for all who kiss the sky, but what about those that do not kiss the sky? Regardless of how much love we hold in our hearts, it is, frankly, impossible to avoid all of the scoundrels, devils, cheats, and swindlers in our day to day life, especially if you live down the street from one of them.

    Despite the fact that this book is dedicated to romance, I thought it would be pertinent to dedicate a chapter to the best ways of dealing with forces that are opposed to love.

The first step, of course, is identifying whether or not you live down the street from a snakeman. Through my studies, I have compiled a list of ten identifying factors. If you answer yes to any six of these warning signs, it is very likely that you are in the presence of a real deal snakeman.

- Unusually high instances of dark magic
- Mean stares
- Cheering and yelling from down the street (Usually during big game)
- Stormy weather
- Fever/Chills
- Suspected devilman gets a new car
- Neighborhood cats and dog become spy-like
- Nearby plants wither and die
- Bad dreams
- Small objects missing or difficult to find

So you're living down the street from a real live scoundrel, what now?

In my own life, I have to deal with a man by the name of Ted Cobbler, a devil who lives down the street and firmly believes that love is not real. Ted stays up all night to party, puts up an unseemly basketball hoop in his driveway, waves hello in a suspicious way and, most damning of all, casts dark magic across the neighborhood.

With such a negative force so close by, it would have been very easy for me to give up on the fight for real love. I will admit that, at times, I nearly have.

However, there is a series of positive affirmations that I've returned to again and again for help, reminders of my sworn mission as a man of real imagination and love.

Included here is a daily reminder for dealing with the snakemen in your own life. This affirmation is spoken aloud in the mirror as a way to remind you of your path for the day, and for your life as whole.

Imagination is real and it is the soul of all special men. Unlike that snake in the grass, Ted Cobbler, I am a special man full of real love and good ways. I am the soul of books. I kiss the sky like the wings of a living billionaire jet plane, stamp the ground like the hooves of a thousand handsome unicorns, ride the flowing waves of life like a ship full of bigfoot pirates, and I have the abs of the worlds cutest dinosaur. I am a cool guy with a slick look, not just a guy with some fries watching for the fun train like that devilman, Ted Cobbler. Love is real.

Using this mantra every day in your own life will provide incredible results, and hopefully one-day drive the snakeman in your neighborhood back to whatever pit they crawled out of.

BIG TIME HOLLYWOOD

I have a friend by the name of Hunter Fox who lives in big time Hollywood, and when my son and me came to visit him, I quickly learned a lot about this strange town. Before I arrived, I always assumed that big time Hollywood was a place of glitz and glamour, which is partially true. However, I quickly learned that the vast majority of big time Hollywood is a deviltown, home to snakes who want nothing more than to destroy real love and romance for all who kiss.

When visiting big time Hollywood, make sure to be prepared for this onslaught of scoundrels. Important items to pack: Spell book, spaghetti, chocolate milk mix, tan screen, hard stare, and big shoes.

Remember that, when entering a deviltown, you are now on a mission to bring real love to all who seek it. Within every deviltown there are always going to be moments of light within the darkness, and you, dear reader, are the bringer of that light.

Warning: If you try to visit these places they will kick you out.

- Buzzfeed office – Angry man says, "No can do, buster."
- Machinima office – Nice ladies, but you can't hang out and snack too long.
- Hollywood Wax Guys – Frozen big timers.
- Park – Devilmen with wolf dogs.

FINAL THOUGHTS

Whether you were looking for help landing that first date with a bigfoot, or trying to decide if the dinosaur you've been seeing for years is truly the right one for you, I hope this book has helped you on your journey.

In my experience as an erotic author, as well as my many years working as a doctor of sensual massage, I have seen all kinds of romance. Love can take many forms, and grow between all creatures of the world with their infinite variations. There is no arguing that love is complicated.

The most important thing to remember though, is that regardless how strange and surreal love can get, no matter how many times the magic of romance can elude you or how often you find yourself confused by the intricacies of sexuality, dating and marriage, one thing is certain above all else. One shining fact remains true no matter where you come from, what color your skin or scales are, or even if your boyfriend is a bus and your girlfriend is a giant cup of coffee.

Love is real.

ABOUT THE AUTHOR

Dr. Chuck Tingle is an erotic author and Tae Kwon Do grandmaster (almost black belt) from Billings, Montana. After receiving his PhD at DeVry University in holistic massage, Chuck found himself fascinated by all things sensual, leading to his creation of the "tingler", a story so blissfully erotic that it cannot be experienced without eliciting a sharp tingle down the spine.

Chuck's hobbies include backpacking, checkers and sport.

Printed in Poland
by Amazon Fulfillment
Poland Sp. z o.o., Wrocław